TABLE OF CONTENTS

For the Teacher

This reproducible study guide to use in conjunction with the novel *Hatchet* consists of lessons for guided reading. Written in chapter-by-chapter format, the guide contains a synopsis, pre-reading activities, vocabulary and comprehension exercises, as well as extension activities to be used as follow-up to the novel.

In a homogeneous classroom, whole class instruction with one title is appropriate. In a heterogeneous classroom, reading groups should be formed: each group works on a different novel at its reading level. Depending upon the length of time devoted to reading in the classroom, each novel, with its guide and accompanying lessons, may be completed in three to six weeks.

Begin using NOVEL-TIES for reading development by distributing the novel and a folder to each child. Distribute duplicated pages of the study guide for students to place in their folders. After examining the cover and glancing through the book, students can participate in several pre-reading activities. Vocabulary questions should be considered prior to reading a chapter; all other work should be done after the chapter has been read. Comprehension questions can be answered orally or in writing. The classroom teacher should determine the amount of work to be assigned, always keeping in mind that readers must be nurtured and that the ultimate goal is encouraging students' love of reading.

The benefits of using NOVEL-TIES are numerous. Students read good literature in the original, rather than in abridged or edited form. The good reading habits, formed by practice in focusing on interpretive comprehension and literary techniques, will be transferred to the books students read independently. Passive readers become active, avid readers.

SYNOPSIS

Thirteen-year-old Brian Robeson is not happy about being the sole passenger aboard a single engine plane going to visit his father in Canada. He is preoccupied with his parents' divorce and the glimpse he had of his mother kissing a man parked in a station wagon at the mall. Suddenly, Brian can no longer afford the luxury of dwelling on his personal problems: the pilot suffers a fatal heart attack. Brian must fly and land the plane alone. Choosing to land the plane over water where there will be less of an impact, Brian manages to bring the plane down and survive the landing. He is bruised, frightened, and alone in the Canadian wilderness.

Besides dealing with terrible thirst and hunger, Brian must learn to understand and live with the wildlife around him. He nourishes himself with wild raspberries and turtle eggs, spears fish, and catches wild birds. Fortunately, Brian has a hatchet, a gift from his mother. With the hatchet he is able to cut wood for a fire, fashion a bow and arrow and a fish spear, and hack his way into the hull of the plane to retrieve the survival kit.

Brian keeps up his spirits by never losing hope that one day he will be found. After fifty-four days of learning the ways of nature and adapting to his new environment, Brian is rescued by a fur buyer looking for trapping camps. Although Brian is grateful to be home, his adventure in the wilderness has had a lasting effect upon him. Not only has he become stronger, but he has also learned to deal with adversity. It has strengthened him sufficiently so that he can now cope with his parents' divorce and the new man in his mother's life.

PRE-READING ACTIVITIES

1. Preview the book by reading the title and the author's name and by looking at the illustration on the cover. What do you think the book will be about? Have you read any other books by Gary Paulsen?

2. What would you include in a survival kit for a small airplane, a camper, a boat, or a car? Make a list of these items and tell the purpose of each.

3. **Cooperative Learning Activity:** Work in a cooperative learning group with several of your classmates. Discuss what it would be like to be stranded alone in the woods. Imagine that it is summertime, yet it is very cold at night. All you have are the clothes on your back and a hatchet. What would you have to do to survive? Fill in the chart below to tell how you would obtain food and shelter, and what you would do to protect yourself from danger. As you read the book, compare your survival strategies to Brian's.

SURVIVAL		
	You	**Brian**
Food		
Shelter		
Protection		

Pre-Reading Activities (cont.)

4. **Social Studies Connection:** On a map locate the northeastern part of the Canadian wilderness, the setting of this book. Do some research to learn about the climate and the plants and trees that grow there.

5. Find stories in newspapers and magazines about people who have survived against incredible odds. Is there any common theme among these stories that shows how people survive? Besides taking care of physical needs such as food and shelter, how do people care for their emotional needs? How do they battle depression and anxiety and reassure themselves that they will be rescued? How would you keep up your spirits if you were lost in the wilderness or were alone at sea awaiting rescue?

6. How does divorce affect children? What do you think parents can do to make it easier for their children when they divorce?

7. **Science Connection:** Find pictures of bears, wolves, moose, skunks, squirrels, and wild rabbits, the animals Brian encounters in the Canadian wilderness. Do some research to learn how these animals adapted to survive in the harsh conditions of their environment. Use the chart below to organize your information.

Animal	Adaptation to Environment
bear	
wolf	
moose	
skunk	
squirrel	
wild rabbit	

CHAPTERS 1, 2

Vocabulary: The following numbered words relate to aviation. Draw a line from each word on the left to its definition on the right. Then use the numbered words to fill in the blanks in the sentences below.

1. altitude
2. cockpit
3. transmitter
4. altimeter
5. compass
6. dashboard

a. control panel in a vehicle
b. instrument that shows how high a plane is flying
c. height of an object above the earth's surface
d. compartment in an airplane where the pilot sits
e. instrument for showing direction
f. equipment that sends out signals

. . . .

1. The _____ told me I was headed west.

2. In his first lesson, the student learned to read all the instruments on the _____.

3. The _____ showed that we were flying high above the clouds.

4. I was invited to sit in the _____ along with the pilot.

5. When the plane was struck by lightning, it quickly lost _____.

6. We flew quickly to the crash site after receiving an emergency message on the _____.

Read to find out what happened to Brian and the pilot on their flight to Canada.

Questions:

1. Why was Brian going to northern Canada?
2. What was still troubling Brian about his parents' divorce?
3. Why was Brian wearing a hatchet in his belt when he boarded the plane?
4. What preparation did Brian have for his emergency solo landing?
5. What strategy did Brian develop for the safest possible landing?

Chapters 1, 2 (cont.)

Questions for Discussion:

1. What memory do you think was troubling Brian?

2. What are some ways that Brian might use his hatchet?

Decision-Making

Brian spends the time between radio transmissions visualizing what will happen when the plane runs out of fuel. This prepares him for what will happen when the plane actually lands. Think of a decision you have to make. On a chart, such as the one below, visualize several alternative courses of action and write the probable results of each.

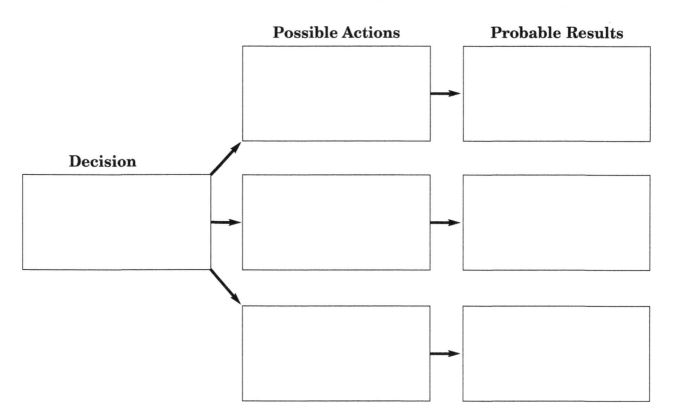

Writing Activity:

Write about a time when you or someone you know had to act quickly in a time of emergency. Describe the situation and its outcome.

CHAPTERS 3, 4

Vocabulary: Synonyms are words with similar meanings. Replace the underlined word in each of the sentences below with its synonym from the Word Box. Write the word you choose on the line below the sentence.

```
                      WORD BOX
      abated       incredible    remnants
      haze         massive       shattered
```

1. The <u>huge</u> bear picked itself up and lumbered over to the campfire.

   _____

2. When the glass <u>broke</u> into a million tiny pieces, we knew it could not be repaired.

   _____

3. The torn <u>pieces</u> of clothing left behind in the woods told us someone had been there.

   _____

4. The young boy told an <u>unbelievable</u> story of his escape from a wild bear in the woods.

   _____

5. We couldn't leave the shelter until the wind and rain <u>diminished</u>.

   _____

6. Through the morning <u>fog</u> we could barely see the trees just ten feet ahead.

   _____

> Read to find out how Brian survived the crash.

Questions:

1. What did Brian do immediately after the plane landed? What happened to him?
2. What was the secret that disturbed Brian?
3. How did Brian feel after the crash?
4. Why did Brian think he was both lucky and unlucky?
5. What did Brian observe in his surroundings?

Chapters 3, 4 (cont.)

Questions for Discussion:

1. Do you think Brian should have kept the secret about his mother to himself or should he have talked to her about what he had seen?

2. What do you think Brian should do first to ensure his survival?

3. What do you think Brian might find in his surroundings to help him survive?

Literary Device: Simile

A simile is a figure of speech in which two unlike objects are compared using the words "like" or "as." For example:

> The memory was like a knife cutting into him. Slicing deep into him with hate.

What is being compared?

_____

What does this reveal about Brian's feelings?

_____

_____

Writing Activity:

Begin a journal for *Hatchet* as though you were Brian. Write about the events as they occur in your reading and express your feelings about what happens.

CHAPTERS 5, 6

Vocabulary: Antonyms are words with opposite meanings. Draw a line from each word in column A to its antonym in column B. Then use the words in column A to fill in the blanks in the sentences below.

A	B
1. murky	a. final
2. frantic	b. negative
3. initial	c. calm
4. obvious	d. increase
5. slender	e. stout
6. positive	f. clear
7. diminish	g. hidden

· ·

1. At first Brian thought his location would be _____ to anyone conducting a search.

2. As each day went by, the pains he suffered as a result of the crash seemed to _____.

3. Brian could not see his reflection in the _____ water.

4. In order to survive, Brian would need to develop a(n) _____ attitude, never giving up hope.

5. When she talked, she gestured with her long, _____ fingers.

6. My _____ reaction was to ignore his complaints, but then I began to realize that he might be right.

7. She made one last _____ plea to be saved.

> Read to find out how Brian created a shelter.

Questions:

1. At first, why did Brian believe he would be rescued soon? Why did he change his opinion?

2. What advice did Brian remember from Perpich, his former teacher? Why was it valuable now?

Chapters 5, 6 (cont.)

3. What did Brian decide was his most immediate need for survival? How did he find something to satisfy that need?

4. Why did Brian establish a shelter near the lake? What kind of shelter did he create?

3–2–1 Review:

Review what has happened so far.

3—Tell three things Brian knows about his situation.

_____

_____

_____

2—Tell two things Brian does not know.

_____

_____

1—Tell one thing that you think Brian will do next.

_____

Questions for Discussion:

Do you think Brian had the skills and the temperament to survive alone in the wilderness? Do you think you could survive in a similar setting?

Writing Activity:

Imagine that Brian was able to send a message on a transmitter to a news reporter. Write a human interest article about Brian that might have appeared in a newspaper. Describe Brian and tell what you know about his location and chance for survival.

CHAPTERS 7 – 9

Vocabulary: Use the context to help you select the best meaning for the underlined word in each of the following sentences. Circle the letter of the word you choose.

1. Once my stomach cramps <u>receded</u>, I was able to continue hiking.

   a. withdrew   b. appeared   c. filled   d. doubled

2. The berries tasted <u>tart</u>, even after we tried to sweeten them with sugar.

   a. sweet   b. sour   c. bland   d. spicy

3. If you <u>gorge</u> yourself at the holiday feast, you will feel sick afterwards.

   a. repeat   b. wash   c. underestimate   d. stuff

4. It became harder and harder to continue the race as the pain in the runner's legs became more <u>intense</u>.

   a. strong   b. quiet   c. wild   d. ticklish

5. Dry wood will <u>ignite</u> more easily than wet wood.

   a. explode   b. char   c. quench   d. light

Read to learn how the hatchet helped Brian survive.

Questions:

1. What memory kept haunting Brian?

2. Why did the raspberries make a better meal for Brian than the gut cherries?

3. How did the bear's behavior surprise Brian?

4. When did Brian first use the hatchet?

5. How did Brian finally get a fire started?

Questions for Discussion:

1. How long do you think Brian could survive in the wilderness?

2. In what ways is Brian changing as he struggles to survive?

Chapters 7 – 9 (cont.)

Cooperative Learning Activity:

Work with a small cooperative learning group to develop two lists: the ways a hatchet could help Brian survive in the wilderness and the ways fire could help. Compare your lists with those of other groups in your class.

Hatchet	Fire

Writing Activities:

1. Write about a time when you or someone you know had to be resourceful to solve a problem. Describe the problem and tell how it was solved.

2. Write about a memory that haunts you in the same way that Brian's memory of his mother affected him. Tell how this memory affects the present.

CHAPTERS 10 – 12

Vocabulary: Analogies are equations in which the first pair of words has the same relationship as the second pair of words. For example: DAY is to NIGHT as EARLY is to LATE. Both pairs of words are opposites. Choose the best word to complete each of the analogies below.

1. CRUDE is to SOPHISTICATED as _____ is to EXTERIOR.
   a. circumference   b. interior   c. surface   d. middle

2. _____ is to TREE as ARM is to BODY.
   a. leaf   b. bark   c. trunk   d. limb

3. DAWN is to SUNRISE as _____ is to TWILIGHT.
   a. dusk   b. morning   c. noon   d. night

4. CIRCLE is to SPHERE as TRIANGLE is to _____.
   a. cube   b. rectangle   c. polygon   d. pyramid

5. SADNESS is to _____ as HILARITY is to HYSTERIA.
   a. silliness   b. fear   c. depression   d. hunger

6. _____ is to ACTIVE as SEARCH is to FIND.
   a. busy   b. dormant   c. emotional   d. fearful

> Read to learn why it was hard for Brian to be optimistic.

Questions:
1. What added responsibility did the fire impose upon Brian?
2. How did tracks in the sand lead Brian to another food source?
3. Why did Brian feel it was important to have things to do?
4. What did Brian mean when he realized his mind and his body had made a connection?
5. Why didn't Brian's spear allow him to capture fish? How did Brian decide to fish instead?

Questions for Discussion:
1. Do you agree with Brian that having things to do can ward off sadness or depression? Has this strategy ever worked for you?
2. Why did the departure of the search plane affect Brian more than if a plane had not come near at all?

Chapters 10 – 12 (cont.)

Literary Device: Personification

Personification is a literary device in which an author grants human qualities to nonhuman objects. For example:

> The eggs had awakened it [his hunger] fully, roaringly, so that it tore at him.

What two objects are personified?

_____

_____

Why is it better than just saying, "Brian was very hungry"?

_____

_____

_____

Writing Activity:

Brian was disappointed when the plane failed to find him. Write about a time when your hope was shattered as Brian's was on this occasion. Tell what you had hoped for, what happened to shatter this hope, and whether your hope has been restored.

CHAPTERS 13 – 15

Vocabulary: Use the context to determine the meaning of the underlined word in each of the following sentences. Then compare your definition with a dictionary definition.

1. After two weeks of rain and cold weather, we <u>exulted</u> in the warmth and sunshine.

   Your definition _____

   Dictionary definition _____

2. The noise of all the birds chirping at sunrise <u>exasperated</u> him to the point of frustration.

   Your definition _____

   Dictionary definition _____

3. When you are ready to shoot the arrow, release the <u>tension</u> on the bowstring.

   Your definition _____

   Dictionary definition _____

4. After being hit in the eye with a hockey puck, Robert worried that he might be permanently blind, or at least visually <u>impaired</u>.

   Your definition _____

   Dictionary definition _____

> Read to learn how Brian has changed.

Questions:

1. What did the narrator mean when he said about Brian, "He was not the same now— the Brian that stood and watched the wolves move away and nodded to them was completely changed."

2. What mistakes did Brian catalog after his first forty-seven days?

3. What was Brian's new "tough hope"?

4. Why did Brian conclude that mistakes had greater significance in the wilderness?

5. How did Brian learn that skunks were neither cute nor funny?

Chapters 13 – 15 (cont.)

6. Why did Brian make a food shelf?

7. How did Brian get his first meat?

Questions for Discussion:

1. What new character traits did Brian now possess that would give him a better chance for survival?

2. What character traits do you possess that might help or hinder your ability to survive in the wilderness?

Science Connection:

Go online and do a search using these keywords — "experiments on refraction of light in water." You will learn why Brian had trouble at first spearing fish in water.

Writing Activity:

Through trial and error, Brian learned about important ways to survive in the wilderness. Based upon what you have read so far, write a list of rules necessary for survival.

Rules for Survival in the Wilderness

CHAPTERS 16 – 18, EPILOGUE

Vocabulary: The English language has many words to express different degrees of a single idea. For example, something that is *torn* may have just one rip; while something that is *tattered* will be ripped in many places. Draw a line from each word on the left to the word on the right that expresses a greater degree of the same idea.

1. pull
2. hungry
3. hit
4. fear
5. damaged
6. shout
7. anger

    a. rage
    b. bellow
    c. starved
    d. battered
    e. slam
    f. panic
    g. wrench

. . . .

Now create your own list of word pairs:

8. thin – emaciated _____
9. hot – _____
10. cold – _____
11. _____
12. _____
13. _____
14. _____
15. _____

> Read to find out how Brian boarded the sunken plane.

Questions:

1. What made Brian realize that nature could be unpredictable?

2. Why was Brian overjoyed to see the tail of the plane sticking out of the water after the tornado?

3. What problems did Brian have to overcome to retrieve the contents of the plane?

Chapters 16 – 18, Epilogue (cont.)

4. What were the most significant items in the survival kit? Why did Brian have mixed feelings about them?

5. How did the pilot discover Brian?

Questions for Discussion:

1. Do you think someone of Brian's age and background could have survived in the wild?

2. What special problems do you think Brian might face as he returns to civilization?

Graphic Organizer:

Use this Venn diagram to show how Brian changed both physically and emotionally from the beginning of the book to the end of the book. Indicate the personality traits that remained the same in the overlapping part of the circles.

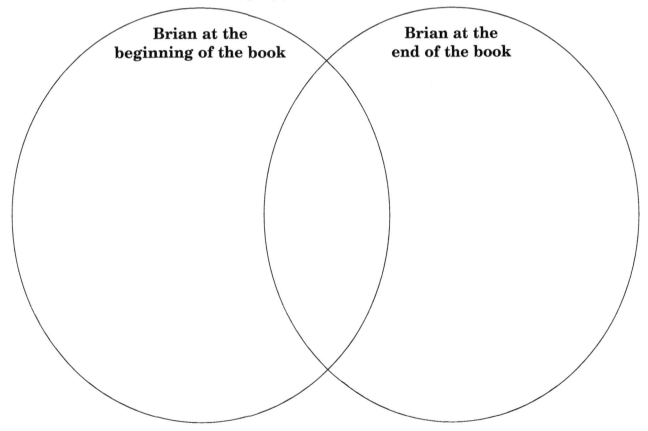

Brian at the beginning of the book

Brian at the end of the book

Writing Activity:

Using the Venn diagram as notes, write about how Brian has changed since the beginning of his adventure. Tell how these changes will affect his relationship with his mother and his ability to deal with the secret that had troubled him.

CLOZE ACTIVITY

The following passage has been taken from the beginning of Chapter Ten. Read it through completely before filling in each blank with a word that makes sense. Then you may compare your language with that of the author.

He could not at first leave the fire.

It was so _____ to him, so close and sweet a _____,

the yellow and red flames brightening the _____ interior of the shelter, the

happy crackle _____ the dry wood as it burned, that _____

could not leave it. He went to _____ trees and brought in as many dead

_____ as he could chop off and carry, _____ when he had a

large pile of _____ he sat near the fire—though it _____

getting into the warm middle part of _____ day and he was hot—and broke

_____ in small pieces and fed the fire.

_____ will not let you go out, he _____ to himself,

to the flames—not ever. _____ so he sat through a long part

_____ the day, keeping the flames even, eating _____ his

stock of raspberries, leaving to drink _____ the lake when he was

thirsty. In _____ afternoon, toward the evening, with his face smoke

_____ and his skin red from the heat, _____ finally began

to think ahead to what he _____ to do.

He would need a large _____ to get through the night. It would

be almost impossible to find wood in the dark so he had to have it all in and cut and

stacked before the sun went down.

POST-READING ACTIVITIES

1. Return to the Cooperative Learning Activity on survival that you began in the Pre-Reading Activities on page two of this study guide. Fill in the column on Brian's survival strategies. Compare them with the survival strategies you recorded before you read the book.

2. Role-play the part of Brian after the rescue. Have another classmate play the role of a reporter interviewing you about your experience in the wilderness. Write out the questions in advance and present the interview to your class.

3. Brian learned a great deal when he lived by himself in the wilderness—how to make fire, how to hunt and fish, how to build a shelter. Although he wouldn't have to use these specific skills once he returned to the city, the knowledge he gained could help him throughout life. How do you think Brian's experience in the wilderness might help him later on?

4. If Brian's rescue had not come before the onset of winter, he would have faced additional problems of survival. What would these problems have been? What are some of the things Brian could have done until the spring thaw?

5. **Art Connection:** Brian's wilderness home is described in great detail in *Hatchet*—the lake streaming with fish, the raspberry bushes, the wildlife. Draw a picture or create a collage, showing Brian's wilderness home with all the objects that helped him survive.

6. Choose another survival book to read. Compare the character in that book to Brian. How were their experiences similar? How were they different? How were the characters similar or different? Compare the way Brian changed to the way the other character changed. Also, compare the settings in the two books. Did different settings require different survival skills?

7. Do you think *Hatchet* would make a good film? If it were made into a film, would you handle the "secret" as part of the sequence of action or as a flashback? Who do you think could play the role of Brian? Are there any scenes you would add, leave out, or change?

8. **Literature Circle:** Have a literature circle discussion in which you tell your personal reactions to *Hatchet*. Here are some questions and sentence starters to help your literature circle begin a discussion.
   - How are you like Brian? How are you different?
   - Do you think Brian is a realistic character? Do you think he faced his challenge of survival in a realistic way?
   - Who else would you like to have read this novel? Why?
   - What questions would you like to ask the author about this novel?
   - I was disappointed when . . .
   - I wonder . . .
   - Brian learned that . . .

SUGGESTIONS FOR FURTHER READING

Defoe, Daniel. *Robinson Crusoe*. Dover.

Ekert, Allan W. *Incident at Hawk's Hill*. Little Brown.

* George, Jean Craighead. *My Side of the Mountain*. Puffin.

* _____. *The Talking Earth*. HarperCollins.

Holm, Anne. *North to Freedom*. Harcourt Brace.

* Holman, Felice. *Slake's Limbo*. Aladdin.

Mathieson, David. *Trial By Wilderness*. Houghton Mifflin.

Mazer, Harry. *Snow Bound*. Laurel Leaf.

McLaughlin, Frank. *Yukon Journey*. Point.

Mowat, Farley. *Lost in the Barrens*. Starfire.

* Nelson, O.T. *The Girl Who Owned a City*. Carolrhoda Books.

* O'Dell, Scott. *Island of the Blue Dolphins*. HMH Books for Young Readers.

* _____. *Julie*. HarperCollins.

* _____. *Julie of the Wolves*. HarperCollins.

Read, Piers P. *Alive*. Avon.

Roth, Arthur. *Iceberg Hermit*. Scholastic.

* Sperry, Armstrong. *Call it Courage*. Simon Pulse.

* Spinelli, Jerry. *Maniac Magee*. Little, Brown.

* Taylor, Theodore. *The Cay*. Laurel Leaf.

* White, Robb. *Deathwatch*. Laurel Leaf.

Some Other Books by Gary Paulsen

Brian's Return. Random House.

* *Brian's Winter*. Ember.

Canyons. Ember.

* *The Crossing*. Scholastic.

Dancing Carl. Simon & Schuster.

* *Dogsong*. Simon Pulse.

The Island. Scholastic.

* *Nightjohn*. Laurel Leaf.

Popcorn Days and Buttermilk Nights. Puffin.

* *The River*. Ember.

Sentries. Simon Pulse.

* *Soldier's Heart*. Laurel Leaf.

Tracker. Simon & Schuster.

Woods Runner. Random House.

Woodsong. Simon & Schuster.

* NOVEL-TIES Study Guides are available for these titles.

ANSWER KEY

Chapters 1, 2
Vocabulary: 1. c 2. d 3. f 4. b 5. e 6. a; 1. compass 2. dashboard 3. altimeter 4. cockpit 5. altitude 6. transmitter

Questions: 1. Brian was going to spend the summer in northern Canada to be with his father who was working on an oil rig. 2. Brian felt that neither his parents, the judge, nor the lawyers had understood his grief over the divorce. Also, he knew something about his mother that he could not discuss with her. 3. Brian's mother gave him a hatchet as a gift to take with him. 4. The only preparation Brian had was the brief lesson in flying that the pilot had given him shortly after take-off. 5. Brian's strategy to land the plane safely was to wait until the plane ran out of gas and then try to bring it down near the shore of a lake.

Chapters 3, 4
Vocabulary: 1. massive 2. shattered 3. remnants 4. incredible 5. abated 6. haze

Questions: 1. After the plane landed, Brian tore himself out of his seat belt and jacket and struggled his way out of the plane and up to the surface of the water. He lost consciousness when he reached land. 2. The secret that disturbed Brian was the memory of his mother kissing a man he didn't know in a station wagon parked at the mall. 3. After the crash, Brian's legs were on fire and his forehead was pounding. He had pain all over. 4. Brian was lucky to have landed where he did and be alive. He was unlucky because of his parents' divorce and because he was stranded in the wilderness. 5. Brian observed that everything was green—a green and blue blur to him. He saw beavers and fish jumping out of the water. There were many different kinds of evergreens. There was a rocky outcropping at the end of the lake that he had luckily missed upon landing.

Chapters 5, 6
Vocabulary: 1. f 2. c 3. a 4. g 5. e 6. b 7. d; 1. obvious 2. diminish 3. murky 4. positive 5. slender 6. initial 7. frantic

Questions: 1. Brian was confident about an early rescue because he knew his parents would search for him immediately, and that the pilot had filed a flight plan. When Brian took over the plane, however, he flew on a different course which would make it more difficult to find him. 2. Brian recalled Perpich's advice to have a positive attitude. Now Brian knew he would have to keep up his spirits in order to survive. 3. Brian needed food first because he was losing strength. Sighting a flock of birds feeding, he found berry bushes. 4. Brian believed if he camped near the lake he would be spotted from the air. He created a shelter at the base of a small bluff that already had three sides, and he built up the fourth side with sticks found on the bank of the lake.

Chapters 7 – 9
Vocabulary: 1. a 2. b 3. d 4. a 5. d

Questions: 1. Brian kept remembering the scene in the mall where his mother kissed the man in the station wagon. 2. The raspberries didn't upset Brian's stomach as the cherries did, and he didn't eat them as quickly. 3. Brian was surprised that the bear left him alone. It ate berries, not people. 4. Brian first used the hatchet when he threw it at an unknown intruder that turned out to be a porcupine. 5. Brian created sparks by rubbing the hatchet blade against the rock. The sparks ignited on birch bark that was shredded to make tinder. Finally, Brian blew gently on the tinder to get a flame started. He fed the flame with wood that he gathered from the ground.

Chapters 10 –12
Vocabulary: 1. b 2. d 3. a 4. d 5. c 6. b

Questions: 1. The fire added to Brian's responsibilities because he had to have sufficient wood to keep the fire going. 2. Brian discovered that the tracks led to turtle eggs, another food source. 3. Brian realized it was important to stay busy because depression diminished when he was active. 4. Brian had become so sensitive to his environment that his mind and his body reacted in unison. He had become acutely aware of new sounds and sights, perceiving things that had changed in a subtle way, and things that could threaten his existence. 5. The fish saw the motion of the spear and swam away. Brian decided to make a bow and arrow in order to fish successfully.

Chapters 13 – 15

Vocabulary: 1. exulted—rejoiced; became overjoyed   2. exasperated—made someone frustrated or angry 3. tension—tightness; tautness   4. impaired—damaged; permanently wounded

Questions: 1. Brian was no longer helpless and self-pitying. He regarded the wolves with respect, but was not overwhelmed with fear, knowing that he could protect himself. 2. The mistakes were using damp or young wood for a fire, almost being blinded when he tried out his first bow, and trying to catch fish without taking into account the refraction of light under water. 3. Brian now believed he could survive on his own whether or not rescue came shortly. 4. Brian believed that mistakes made in the wilderness had greater significance because they could have fatal consequences. In the city there were usually ways to rectify mistakes. 5. Brian, trying to protect his buried turtle eggs from a skunk, received a direct spray to his eyes. This left him blinded for two hours and in pain for two weeks afterwards. 6. Brian made a food shelf because he needed to store food for a time when he might be unable to obtain it and the storage place had to be high enough so the food would be safe from animals. 7. Brian finally obtained his first meat when he successfully speared a foolbird. He cleaned the bird and cooked it over his fire.

Chapters 16 – 18, Epilogue

Vocabulary: 1. g 2. c 3. e 4. f 5. d 6. b 7. a; Answers to the rest of the vocabulary activity will vary.

Questions: 1. Brian realized that nature could be unpredictable when the moose attacked and the tornado hit. 2. Brian was glad to see the plane because he remembered there was a survival kit on it. 3. Brian had to build a raft to get to the middle of the lake, make cord to hold it to the plane, hack his way inside the plane, and dive to the bottom of the lake to retrieve his dropped hatchet. 4. The rifle and the butane lighter were the most significant items in the survival kit. Brian felt good that he would not have to struggle to light a fire or capture game. The lack of these luxuries, however, had made Brian more resourceful and at one with his environment. He would miss that feeling. 5. The pilot discovered Brian after picking up a message on the transmitter and then spotting the plane in the lake.